Dust of Angels

Dust of Angels

Poems by HARRY WAITZMAN

Leapfolio
an imprint of Tupelo Press

NORTH ADAMS, MASSACHUSETTS

Library of Congress Catalog-in-Publication data available upon request.
[ISBN: 978-1-936797-78-3]

Cover designed by Sarah Russell.
Cover photo: "Horizon Study" by Jeffrey Levine, used with permission of the artist.

FIRST PAPERBACK EDITION: NOVEMBER 2015.

Leapfolio, an imprint of Tupelo Press
Post Office Box 1767
North Adams, Massachusetts 01247
Telephone: (413) 664–9611
editor@tupelopress.org
www.tupelopress.org.

For my wife Marcia and mentors Thomas Lux, Mark Doty, Jill Hoffman, and Sharon Dolin.

Contents

PART I

Let the marbles roll in life's game of chance,
while genes control, we still need "mazel."

Stranger in Congers

Seven bars, four churches, no library.
An old-timer rummages through garbage cans.
I steal a neighbor's *New York Times*
thrown on the morning lawn.
The funeral parlor is the local hangout.

The waiting room of the railroad station
blooms with bulbs, mowers and rakes,
Burpee seeds and plastic owls.
Fog paints the eaves of the white houses
on Burnside and Sheridan Streets.
No one remembers the Union generals
the streets were named for.

A bent hickory sways in the back yard,
I want to climb its trunk to build a tree house.
Our apple tree is home
to a thousand tent caterpillars.
Summer's white lilacs beckon, purple sumac
invites my hands to crush the berries.

The mailman walks by and scowls,
whistling, he fills all mailboxes but mine.
Every dog on the block tries to bite me.
Young women no longer flirt in the supermarket.
No one keeps my telephone number.
I'm in serial remission; Congers opens
its blue doors while a steam engine
whistles to Hoboken.

The Zoo Between My Ears

The frog in my bathtub blinks at me.
In my bed the snake rattles hello.
I can't sleep because I itch all over—
my pillow is a two humped camel.

Sleepwalking after midnight,
I bump my head on a door left open,
and the trunk of an elephant,
so hairy and insinuating, makes me sneeze.

Stumbling into the living room a rhino
lunges while monkeys swing from the
chandelier. The cleaning woman does a
sloppy job, but she doesn't break things,

my wife says, so I can't blame the
monkeys on the maid, still every time
someone leaves the front door ajar
the zoo grows by degrees.

I will move to the Congo and live
under a palm tree. There I will bathe
when the river floods. Happy is the man
whose crocodiles swim out of doors.

Two Pens

I hammer my thoughts into words
and in the hammering, make poems loud,
clear and resonant.

We must write with two pens.
One is not enough,
one may be stolen, the other lies or distorts
truths and flags false revelations.

Our tongues must rise up and flee past tides
of public opinion. Trust no waves of reassuring
facts. These are false advertisements.

Instead, temper your complaints, love freely.
Death collects every penny of your life.

Country Lawyer

I speed over leaf-splattered streets,
frighten squirrels and park under court
house trees. After dragging my body to the Tor
Luncheonette, I swish cups of coffee
and converse with buddies.

My airway whistles, soothing litigious bones.
I bounce from law books to black telephones,
dictate the Louisiana Purchase and cancel
the sale of Manhattan Island. Before lunch,
I must talk to Lincoln about speculation
in Western lands.

Autobiography

I chase the brown squirrels
into forgotten woods and they stare at me,
holding chestnuts in their paws
as if they were my past.

My mind turns glossy pages of three
alumni magazines, Penn, Columbia, and Sarah
Lawrence, all after money.

I read about the triumphs of strangers
and the passing of friends
not forgotten, my brothers in obituaries.

To be young again,
with shoelaces tied neatly
and hair brushed grey to my temples.

A minor poet from a small county,
I sometimes rage and sometime love
too much—the woman in the red dress
who speaks French and Mandarin—
and my wife of so many years
who speaks Portuguese and who
knows what else.

A difficult man stuttering without tears,
who knows appearances count,
that squirrels are rats with bushy tails.
I'm a mouse among men,
a robin below eagles, a lone crow
who caws at condors.

Yellow Pike, Whitefish, Buffle & Carp

Father has a rainbow curving over
his head, that descends from a shout of clouds,
a drum of oaths, the store shaking with gills
and heaps of sawdust soaking blood.

Yellow pike, whitefish, buffle and carp,
glisten in a second life. Father boasts
his fish smell like fresh cucumbers.

Slicing the pike, he swears in Yiddish
and puts on a show for customers
who in babushkas, load
their bundles into baby carriages.

With a wooden clopper, he hits live carp,
their eyes popping, soft mouths clenching air,
tails whacked skywards, bladders bursting,
bloody slime flowing along pine counters.

I get gut in my eye and slime on my cheeks.
Fish scales stick to my tongue and fins wiggle
in my mouth. Father bellows from his throne,

"Mixed fish, fresh fish, all you can eat.
Good weight, 25 cents a pound."
I cower below a wooden shelf.

On holidays he allows me to take cash.
I cry I want to be a fish-man like him,
and he laughs, "you will become
a doctor-lawyer."

I Place My Ear to the Ground of Congers

I feel the vibrations
of a Baldwin steam engine
pounding rails,
all brass and whistles,
the blue-capped engineer waving,
the fireman crouching low, shoveling coal,
seven hours to the yards in Buffalo.

A rowboat sleeps, water up to the gunwales.
Oars move like pickerels under lilies,
waves licking the shore
while frogs and sunfish wiggle into sight.
I squash a bug. If it turns out to be
a hornet, I will scoot to the water
for cooling mud to soften the pain.

I try to counterfeit coins,
placing old pennies
on the track, waiting for the press
of wheels to make them nickels.
I become an airplane over the meadow
and soar and glide to haystack landings.
I suck on timothy grass toothpicks,
spit green and whistle for my dog Spots
to stop romancing a neighbor's collie.

Father says, there's a war coming.
And I ask, where, when? He says,
over the ocean, the Germans again.
Remembering the Huns from a history
class, I'll be ready to enlist at 17.

But not yet, instead, I bike
to my girlfriend's house.
We walk and I pinch her bottom,
she screams loud as cow bells,
and hits me hard, angry as a hornet;
mud doesn't help.

On a Spring Valley Farm

From deep within her bovine lungs
our only cow remembers my name
and sings a song to Harry
as her calf pokes her teats.

When the April sun frees our pasture,
yellow forsythia whip my face
and underbrush grabs my ankles.

In the barn the hired hand teaches me
solitaire and tells me:
see the rain running down the leg
of your rooster. Don't be like that.

From the Dog House

I tell Father
"Life is short, grandchildren
make it longer." He calls me
the "groise filosophe"
though I'm only eight.

I compete for affection
with Plato our neighbor's dog.
He barks and bites
as I wrestle and love him
because Mom won't let me
keep a dog.

Our next door neighbors
are Greek and nice.
They give me a nickel
each week to buy ice cream
from the Good Humor man.

The years are simple and fun
before I start to study geometry.
Euclid's curves and arcs confuse me.
There is no end to the angles
of my despair.

The rise and fall of history is easy
to learn. Maybe I don't remember
who Herodotus was, but you can't help
but love that name, and if I had a dog,
that's what I'd call him.

The Bananas on the Top of the Fridge

Count the brown spots as they ripen.
The clock sweeps past midnight.
I toss and groan, get up at 3 o'clock,
peel half, eat half, dream.

In a dense swamp in Costa Rica
a fer-de-lance nests as I sleep.
Its swollen tongue flutters and grazes my ear.
I wake to a female jaguar licking my toes.
She hears her kittens cry and pads her way
back to a lair of rotting tree trunks.

These lines come from an emerald river
inside my head. Delivered with slaps
on the back, a baby starts bawling, hungry,
wanting bananas, too.

On June 3

I celebrate another birthday.
Days and weeks commit small treasons
against my body. Soon I will swing
from memory's gallows.

I brace myself, no time to tuck in loose
corners or to untwist kinks and knots.
Put a hand to my crotch and mirror
to my mouth. He jogs across my path.

Strange fires warm my hands, strange fires bake
loaves of bitter bread. I dip my hands into the flames.
I look up to the mountain and my hands are cooled.
Climbing to Jerusalem, balm falls on my head.

Strawberry Ice Cream

In my red Ford Explorer,
my left hand has the feel of the road,

right foot easy on the gas,
in the passing lane, life speeds by.

As a thousand times before,
I cross the reservoir, scattering geese

on the causeway, plowing through
the wind, Hi Tor whistling down at me.

Congers Lake Road curves past an
old Dutch home with a wide stoop

and sandstone chimney. Stumps
of trees remain, no pigsties survive.

Leaf blowers deafen with their insistence.
The West Shore freight streaks

through Congers, red lights stalling
everything but the years.

Condo with Weathervane

Once I stuffed a frog in a bottle
and tried to revive it with prayer.

When it stopped breathing, I cried
and buried it in the cemetery of ants.

I stumble on stones in an old pasture and feel
cold quartz pebbles carried by a glacier.

Before milking time of brown cows
in red barns, I swat mosquitoes bleeding my arm.

Their blood mingles with mine, we are kindred
fellows and lowly worms earn my embrace.

The tin rooster crows every morning,
waking my cows at milking time.

The Swans at Congers

The lake spreads out before my eyes
to Hi Tor's stone buttresses,
water without waves, a giant mirror
reflecting the opposite shore.

Grey elephant clouds march across
the sky, trumpeting tomorrow's storm.
Slick water slides over the dam,
spilling into Hackensack.

A boy with rod casts for a future,
angling from the reservoir road. No bass,
only dust as cars barrel by. He goes home
empty handed, back to the job at the mill

for a minimum wage. The birthing storm
roils the broken green glass. I hear the cries
of geese as water breaks into silver slivers.
I swim upstream into Yeat's Celtic sadness,

to my own reservoir where wild swans throng.
Far from Ireland except in banter and voices
of men crowding the Irish bars of Congers,
their tongues dressed in the ancient brogue.

Swans explode in Lake Deforest, white against green.
The yet harsher light of envy betrays me.

Mourning the past, I fear next morning's storm
and sketch the face of the ravaged mountain
after explosions toss trap-rock into barges.

My hamlet survives, the railroad sings a song,
the clickety-clack of what will happen.

PART II

The roof and the wall collapse in flame and heat seizes the foundations.
Now there is only earth, sandy, trodden down,
with one leafless tree.

— Czelaw Milosz
A Poor Christian Looks at the Ghetto
(trans., Milosz)

The Stone Sentinels of Prague

Walking slowly in the old Jewish cemetery
to see the tombstones crouch. Centuries
have fallen on them, they are deep in sleep,
only a few are restless under their blanket of leaves.

With a willow stick, I touch carved headstones
speaking with gestures, pointing
to Hebrew names remembered in worn rock.
They survive with loving inscriptions,

dates of birth and death, their trades
the names of spouses. They groan and sweat,
grass and granite are their companions.
Without breath, they suck air in from my lungs.

The ghetto's dumb soldiers eat rain and slush
and pack snow in their knapsacks. On the midnight
watch, icicles fall from linden trees and wake them.
When pogroms piss blood on Prague's cobbled

streets, they bark like dragons and eat glass -
I salute Horovitz and Gans who defended
congregations in Bohemia when Adam's apples
bobbed on stakes. I inspect the ranks, so Jewish,

so out of line, talking back to corporals, almost
to G-d. Even on Shabbat, smoke creeps
through the ranks, where in full view, a bald
trooper empties his bladder against a tree.

What is there to tell the soldiers in the cemetery
behind the Altneuschus? My friend Karpeles grins, he pcints
to his campaign ribbons, wants a promotion.
His belly sags and bandaged feet stink to heaven.

The Dybbuk from Delancey Street

Hovering above cobbled streets, I catch
sparks struck by hooves and stuff them in my
mouth. Like raisins, flames sweeten my tongue.

Sweat rides on my brows and rolls
into my eyes. I come down to dampen dreams
of greenhorns smoldering in the gutter,

fanned by nimble fingers and broad backs. I roam
unattached as Spirit in a world of nails and thongs.
Undecided upon the lure of evil, sure of the pain

of good, I look for lost souls to cling to
and find a junk man plodding along the docks
gathering the cream of garbage cans.

Morning light furls the flag of a steamship
newly arrived from Hamburg with a cargo
of lathes and presses, Jews and Poles

in steerage and babies dry heaving
from dehydration. Tubs of soup, prayers,
revive them. I meet the driver of a wagon

who rests his whip and tells how cholera
flares along the East River, maybe from India.
I open water mains and flood the streets.

In a cold-water flat, built by speculators, almost
windlowless on an Alphabet street, a child is born.
A nurse tends delivery in a steaming kitchen.

The father, a carpenter, is out of work, the Panic
of '93 lingers. After circumcision, the baby screams,
the mother's sewing machine sings past bedtime.

I'm roused by tin bells clinking and a junk man
in a top hat yelling, "Old clothes, old clothes."
Torn suits, broken shoes, corsets are tossed.

From diphtheria-plagued tenements,
I walk by the cross-eyed and beautiful, past
a portly beggar with T.B., and pickpockets

with fat fingers and enter a building where coughs
echo in hallways and Norwegian rats parade up
coal chutes. I remove the sign, Quarantined.

I meet a kindred spirit seeking victims and boast,
"Joe's kid died yesterday from a fever the health
nurse couldn't diagnose. When the last breath

slipped out, I touched Joe's lips, entering his body
under the cover of grief. Now he screeches prayers like
a parrot and walks in torn clothes, blaming himself.

At the funeral he howls like a wounded animal."
On Sunday the sin of disease is chastised from
marble pulpits uptown. Dirt is excoriated.

Immigrants packed ten to a bed are blamed
for epidemics. The infant's life was brief, his death
unnoticed, the grave one by two feet,

bought cheap, between two thieves
dug in the cemetery section where crickets
don't chirp and headstones tilt.

Joe and I sway on a low mourning bench.
His shrieks become my shrieks and grab my throat.
We wrestle in smoke and stink, unseen by

sweaty, bearded faces. I stumble over a rebbe
praying in the dark as Joe drifts in and out of focus,
his speech blurred, then sharp as a broken glass.

The dusty room glows luminous, charged by
the current anxious thoughts. Why do my palms
sweat when I'm inside a body? The rebbe's hands

tremble, he claps for a miracle, Joe's eyes roll,
his arms flail in the air. I feel his heart explode in
his chest. He falls gagging, I breathe air into his

mouth and his thrashing subsides, the blue
in his eyes returns. He looks around and sobs
as his world folds into a plain pine box.

I leave hungry and tired, as if my bones
were rendered into a soup of tears for those
seized by the madness of empty plates.

I'm the Dybbuk of Delancey Street, unable
to cast spells in the New World. Lumbago
cramps my attempts at simple witchcraft.

In Gehenna, my father disowns me, ashamed
I bear his name and I'm left to earn my keep
behind a pushcart, peddling notions and shoelaces.

In the old country, spun heads and twisted minds.
In Kiev, I dealt in fits and gilded nightmares.
On this cold night, I stamp my feet on Orchard Street

and sell the eye of a needle to a blind man and air
in soap bubbles to children. After dark, I hawk
hunger and lust for pearly tits to sailors prowling

dance halls on the Bowery. After midnight, factory
smoke rubs against my body. Soot covers my head,
I join the Devil's minyan. My head grows grid marks

from sleeping under the Brooklyn Bridge. Spider
light slants through the latticework and stains my
curbstone pillow. Fire and salt preserve me.

Joe returns from the land of lean faces where hope died.
His friends gather and remove the sheets on mirrors.
Soon Joe's wife laughs again at her husband's silly jokes.

Their secret, a child quickens within the wife's womb.
Her belly balloons like the sun rising over Greenpoint.
Joe saws new leaves for the Passover table. Elijah comes.

Tea with Milosz

On September 1, 1939 Germany invades Poland

Meet a fishmonger from Lodz,
who pickles herring in salt-stained
oak barrels. These silver fish,

tasty, invigorating with a baked
potato and half-baked Jewish humor,
whose fish are my fish.

Have some black bread, Milosz, and herring
before night falls and all of Europe
sinks into war.

Join me for a glass of tea
with my last cube of sugar.
How wind from the Steppes bakes

man and beast this September
morning. I try to cool off in Danzig Park,
as sparks fly my mouth.

Stranger, we meet by chance
on a park bench in Danzig,
Poland's gooseneck to the sea.

I travel to Prussia from Lodz
with a caravan of fish, selling
tidbits to herring lovers.

Last week as I slept soundly
in Poznan, kids stole the front
wheels from my wagon and painted

my horse sun-yellow. I rubbed
her nose, gave her some carrots,
made new wheels.

Above the linden trees, crows of the Reich soar
their iron wings with swastikas unfurled above
church spires and my herring cart.

The pig is out of the pen again,
its body longs to wallow in our streets,
chew with its snout on our street lamps.

Milosz, the guns of the "Schleswig-Holstein"
are frightening the gulls in Danzig harbor
and already coffin makers sharpen their tools .

Our Polish cavalry will charge German tanks
with plumed sharp lances.
Our land so flat, so inviting.

2.

Boiling water in a Samovar
the fishmonger talks to Milosz

Zubrovka, the yellow vodka flavored
with buffalo grass my friends call buffalo piss
makes drunks of peasants and princes;

Milosz, we live near shuls in the shadow
of marble cathedrals but our prayers carry
to heaven without incense.

We cough our way to altars, sweating
and speak simply to G-d, asking
for a new kingdom for our children.

Boruch Hashem!
for black hats and green brides
who ripen into buxom women.

The toothy bride queen for the evening:
May G-d bless this union with a dozen children;
flapping diapers will be flags of her kingdom.

Papa dances barefoot at the banquet hall,
stomping on notes of a wheezing accordion,
wild as the handsome bull in the red barn

that services five cows every morning.
O the *simchas* of a shtetl! Our fur-hatted rebbe jumps up
on a pine table and splits his black trousers down the middle.

3.

Czelaw, take two sugar cubes
to sweeten my bitter story.

Milosz, we must not quarrel with the clock.
These poor Polish horses will take us
part of the way to the fires of our comrades.

We still have time, pour the hot water,
let tea leaves swim in the cup.
Sip and watch the sun set

over bones of Teutonic knights
and ragged Polish cavalry.
All sleep uneasy under Baltic dunes.

Chirps of sparrows scratch the bronzed horizon,
edging lines between purple clouds
and amber laden waters.

Silver herring fatten, Jutland's
dreadnoughts rust and Dover sole
glide beneath hooks and nets.

4.

BMW Motorbikes with Sidecars Halt in the Square

Give me another glass of tea; our tongues unwind
and turn the clock back. We must go underground.

Milosz, the samovar's empty.
Swastikas are filling village squares.
I see your poems as pennants on medieval
lances. Polish cavalry charge German tanks
in 1939. Your poems are more lethal,
the words twist like bayonets, poetry
as minefield. If the poet is Milosz,
the ghetto survives in your scribbling

in sewers, in the company of learned rats,
the last survivors of the Warsaw ghetto
who breathe to this day and recite
kaddish and mass for all, in graves

covered by cobblestones, wisps of dust,
chips of bone, Poles, Jews, circumcised,
or not, homosexuals, gypsies, prelates
and rabbis, in an underground cathedral
built from coal pillars, columns of salt,
catacombs where rats congregate,
whiskers quivering.

A flume cuts across ice in the meadow,
ash covers the village and whitens roofs.
In the valley of the Shoah, flesh and bone
grow into flowers, grass is bent in mourning.

The Dust of Angels

Milosz, smoke rises from stoves in our D.P. Camp
as showers spritz water on kids.

We pack memories in cardboard valises,
embrace and say "Shalom,"
leaving our friend the samovar for others
to heat. It was our battered companion
for a thousand nights and kept us from freezing.

Six letters were painted on the hull
of a salt-streaked ship plotted to overcome
waves and the blockade of the British.
A new Exodus begins over impatient seas.

Graveless bodies dance atop the ship's holds
whirling on shoulders of survivors.
The old steamship crosses the Mediterranean,
this new ark brings remnants to the Holy Land,
not lions or giraffes but survivors with children.

The dust of angels is laid to rest in Poland's fields
behind barbed wire and Gates of Hell.
Once the tracks to Auschwitz clacked death
as inmates garbed in stripes were rounded up
into rooms awaiting G-d's breath.

The earth renews itself in the wash of diapers,
the cries of babies and kites of the young.
Early spring's twigs unfurl impatient buds.
Tassels of corn hoist June's green flag,
the rails to Auschwitz rust,
a thousand nights, keep us from freezing.

PART III

Lee Krasner, Revolutionary

A pile of horse manure steams opposite
a stoop in East New York as a sparrow lands
and warms its wings on the glistening mass.

A bird pecks away until full.
There is beauty in the golden mound,
and smells, vibrant, overpowering.

With a clop, clop "der ferd un roiter vogen"
sways carrying ice sold in blocks for pennies.
The iceman grins at well-scrubbed children.

Lee has no easy ladder from modest means,
talent may climb a thousand steps to nowhere,
her brush explodes in surprising ways.

She splashes color against the canvas
of her life and dances with her brush
as her palette makes lines of charcoal shiver.

No academic, she grinds the nerves
of monocled critics and exposes
the turmoil of inner self.

Standing at the barricades, tall and impetuous,
her paintings scrape dull perspective into oblivion
and consign bowls of fruit to the refrigerator.

Her paintings radiate bright as dawn or dark as
midnight crowned by the moon. Pay her no homage,
from a distance, but close up inside bones of her work.

Let the paint
                drip
        as if it's
                    leaking
from a wound.

Georgia O'Keefe's Alien Corn

Tarantulas time her daily departure
in a Model A Ford to paint the hills.
A lone crow follows her
into the wilderness.

She makes a garden of bones
in the desert. Her portable easel
frightens no one. Mountain
lions become her friends.

The bliss of snakes enshrines
the place where she paints.
She plucks the heart of alien corn
that ripens as a sacrifice.

In July O'Keefe's dark corn
sucks clouds dry. Wind whistles
through eye sockets of skulls
forever bone in the desert.

Rembrandt on Canal Street

I am so homesick for Amsterdam.
The Dutch names, the Bowery,
Coenties Slip soothes me.

I'm at home on the streets and docks.
How could we lose to the British?

We paint better. Our women
spread their legs wider …

Our tulips bloom like milkmaids,
pink and yellow and supple.

I cannot find a single, decent round of Edam,
ditto fat herrings in oak barrels.

I paint blue graffiti on alley walls.
I walk with Saskia and find seats at a cafe.

She joins me in America, full bellied,
anxious about our first child.

Picasso's Broken Mirror

I gather flowers, pigments,
pebbles, broken glass and spread them out
on a mirror in a studio in Paris.

I break the mirror and toss the shards
on my palette, women's faces turn pink,
bodies have gashes pubic brown.

Women should be treated differently.
I love them all and prepare to ink
dancing buttocks, gathering rosebuds
of flesh for a lithograph.

My ears hear the rumble of bones. I lift the skirt
of a woman and her pelvis becomes a cradle.

Whitman Beholds the Brooklyn Bridge

At the Bowery and Canal, Walt sells newspapers.
When no one buys late news of Grant's push
into the Wilderness, he quits,

hunts for "reb" caps in dinky pawn shops,
stumbles along Pike Street, where last year
caissons sank into the East River.

The Bridge looms above, suspended
by democratic curves of cable.
The quiet strength and daring in Roebling's steel.

Beyond Manhattan's docks, he imagines
the bridge turns fuzzy, stretches like caramel,
its cables snapping like the breaking of harp strings.

The last copy of the *Eagle* sells out
to commuters heading for Brooklyn Heights
on the Fulton Ferry. America prospers.

He doesn't live to see the dock reborn
as a fish market. The Bridge still glides
on its wings across the river.

Soho

The sparse plane trees on Thomson Street,
trunks surrounded by dog shit blossom anyway,
Norwegian maples drown in piss,
dropping leaves prematurely,

a reminder we don't really need or want,
and in spite of which, I speed down the parkway
from the suburbs, paroled for an afternoon,
leaving a wife with a four-wheel-drive social life.

Past a sign reading "Deer Crossing," a young
woman jumps from the woods, naked
firm breasts moving like a deer's antlers,
cream colored hips blurred into her rump.

No stopping now, I accelerate my flight to Soho.
I want to ramble around galleries, searching
for young artists, unheralded by critics but so fine,
so affordable. At street corners, Japanese

and German conversations hang like kites in the air.
Galleries carved out of warehouses poke light
on carved granite sidewalks. I'm invited
to climb iron stairs, to view soft sculptures

of woolen balls of yarn and metal works fashioned
of bashed fenders. I prefer the feel of bumpers
and of brass standpipes sprinkled down every street.

Then, like a gunpoint hold-up, a tall, sturdy figure,
polychrome Kouros, sculpted by Manuel Neri,
the ancient Greek form partly painted, part naked stone,
archaic man imprisoned!

On the New Jersey Turnpike, I Stopped to Pee
at the Walt Whitman Service Center near Camden

On Sunday afternoon parking wasn't easy, the entrance
crowded, would I make it? On the wall leading to the
men's room, three poems and a photo of Walt's were
framed and hung, possibly to inspire and educate the
pissers. I forget the poem's names. I was in a rush.
But words like "democracy," "Modern Man" stood out.
I unzipped my fly and stood facing an electronic urinal.
I heard sounds

of cavalry, horse dongs hosing a meadow and the echo
of yawps from boys dying with Walt's hand on their
fevered brows. I left saluting the portrait of a man
with his hat a rakish angle, his beard curling from a
friendly chin, everybody's grandfather who fathered
a thousand poets who joined up and charged into the
future when his bugle blared.

Stalin's Mustache

I wish I were Russian,
like the poet Osip Mandelstam
our too brief companion,
killed for pointing out
cockroaches in high places.

Instead, I close the Venetian blinds
to keep out the darkness.
I'm a fly in the chicken soup
drowning in fat, drifting
on a sprig of parsley.

Here in America we need
a new revolution every week.
We've become crocodiles,
eat our children then complain
we're childless.

Goya's Copper Plates

Ink splashes and pools on the copper plate,
defines the wings and face of a demon.

Paper is pressed against the metal and a monster
rouses itself from copper and flies off, all beating wings.

Goya rests for the afternoon, tired of harrowing
beasts who dart around his head. He yells, more

ink, more paper, he's not done. The sky must be
filled with flapping lizards and prey, as ever in his mind.

He must grow horns and charge
red-eyed over the Pyrenees.

He must sharpen the teeth
of his friends, enlarging their scaly wings

so they fly still higher, still faster
to master their prey.

To My Accomplice, Charles Baudelaire

My own flowers of evil bloom where river rats
congregate and bite my toes.

I walk over a cast-iron bridge, staring
through fog at satanic waves.

A prostitute greets me and for a few sou
offers her wares. She calls it love.

Turning my back I lift the Seine high
over my head. I am dizzy, penniless.

My songs unheard.

Gustav Klimt and Adele

The Neue Galerie in New York
lowers its lights a whole century.

Small indiscretions everywhere,
necklines, the royalty of genius and flesh.

My eyes unhook the straps of her gown
and her neck, Oh Grecian pillar! rests

upon velvet shoulders. I touch her nipples,
blood rushes the color of ripe peaches.

My eyelashes brush her pale stomach,
a pearl of warm flesh undulating,

then that tide rushes as if oysters
had lost their grasp on the seabed,

swirled into a feast
of succulence and salt.

Stooping low I trace the blue veins
of her thighs. The faintest scent

lifts, mingled with the French perfume
behind her ears, her shoulders. Her shoulders.

Intoxicated, I reel into her arms
to steady myself, descending into flesh.

Fireflies and Kimonos

Seated on my throne in the bathroom,
I watch butterfish nibble on wallpaper.
Above the mirror, red bream swim a
through a coral reef. In "A Shoal
of Fishes," Hiroshigi paints the rhythm

of finned life where pearl divers reach
to make necklaces, pulling our eyes
to their cleavage, a radiant breath
around their necks and even poisonous fugu
live in an honorable place.

I sit without tail or gills, naked,
ingesting water, expelling bubbles.
The Japanese revere octopus and eel,
bow to Fujijama, pray for long life, for cicadas
to sing forever, for kimonos always to open.

Reparations for a Wife

"I bought myself the Goya print, buy yourself
the cashmere robe." My wife smiles at my voice
as I try to sound commanding.

One purchase balances another,
keeps my marriage from shivering,
and later on I whistle in the bathroom

tuning out the nicks and cuts
hardened to the edge of vows.
There is revolution in the air

and blood of the Peninsular War congeals
on my gullet, and as I shave Napoleon gives
Josephine a tiara as reparations.

PART IV

"Heh, Professor! We have Happy Bass, best cheapest
fish in Chinatown. Steam with bok choy for dinner."

In Early Spring

Ice chokes the lazy brooks, streams
thaw and unwind across the meadows.

At the lily pond I cup my hand over a waterbug,
my big toe bait for a tadpole.

I'm the birdman quiet as a hawk
winging over the hen house.

Rhode Island Reds are friendly,
White Leghorns snooty.

My buddies are feathered and noisy
and crowd around me when I feed them.

I'm careful not to step on skunk cabbage
whose pale white flowers parade

through the swamps and bite your nose
when you pick them.

Our only cow remembers
my name and lows

a song to Harry from the depths
of her bovine lungs.

Survival Hardware

My sledgehammer tongue whacks the world,
one, two, three times a day,

evening and morning, my eyes
paint the world green.

No reason, each day gives us chances,
you win some and lose some,

so I would butt like a billy goat and piss
on the moon every month, happily giving it color.

Tiger Dream

The moon stopped rising.

The sun froze in its tracks.

Geese flew upside down.

Trees grew branches

under their roots.

I tossed unable to sleep.

My son chalked equations

like Einstein. He played

the violin like a virtuoso.

He jumped ten feet over the zoo fence

and spoke Chinese to a tiger.

I cut through steel bars with my teeth

and make love to the tiger's keeper.

Dutch Gardens

This morning, I forget my hat and coat
and leave my wife alone in my condo

and go to rest on a bench in Dutch Gardens
behind the Court House.

I count my heartbeats and breaths
per minute.

Is my new pacemaker
behaving while I doze?

I rise and kick off my shoes
and spread my arms like a bird.

My body pirouettes on sharp pebbles
of the gravel path.

I dance between puddles
and asphalt

and shake my fist
at the sun.

Zebra

I nibble tufts of grass in the savannah
where ants greet me, the ones who build
apartment houses and high-rises.

Behind bars or peering above them,
I squint at females of every species:
hairy, bald, proudly hyena.

Here is the shape of desire:
conical breasts beneath ample shoulders,
copper rings circling stretched necks,

hips that move quietly like sand dunes,
a friendly oasis between long legs,
breath that chimes like night music.

Mozart and I play games in the park.
He roars with the timbre of genius
and rolls hoops to his sister Maria.

Mine is dead almost ten years.
O Sylvia, Sylvia.
I miss your mistakes on the piano.

In the jungle, your kid brother
plays the violin without you,
making mistakes of my own.

Fly in Amber

I wiggle myself free, my wings
delicate and reflecting light.

Admirers pass my nose but I'm not noticed.
I'm lost in the serenity of amber,

my thorax at peace, my buzz
turned off. The sun

no longer bejewels resin
in ancient trees along the Baltic

but shines on the amber pendant
worn by my love.

The attraction is electric.
I press my cheek to her ancient breast.

On my 80th Birthday

Dry is the pumpernickel of my youth.
Once hot slices slabbed with sour cream burned
the roof of my mouth and red borscht and ripe
cherries stained red the vest of my bar mitzvah suit.

I smell pine boards drying in a kiln ready to be pegged.
Angels hum in heaven as they weave tachrichim.
I dance atop an unopened grave, my unpeopled coffin,
celebrating my 80th birthday.

I pray for my health, for my bladder
and my colon and all of the other vital parts
and pieces of my body. Mornings, I intone the prayers
every observant Jew has said for six thousand years
and change.

On waking, I clear my head with cold splashes of water.
At twilight, I pray my six grandchildren will grow tall,
straight, and observant.

Thunder in April

My mouth smokes, my fingers tingle,
snow drifts around Rockland Lake.
Hungry muskrats lick their paws and sniff,
while fishermen cut holes in the ice,
light fires and camp on the wet, white grass.

The sun mows the sparkling blades.
Mud puddles on the shore, rivulets run.
After one thunderstorm, another loud clap
wakes everything sleeping on South Mountain.

Pickerels stir, sneaking past lilies towards minnows.
Skunks browse like brazen politicians, fearing no one.

Tea with Slices of Lemon

Darjeeling; darling. There is no solace
in croissants. Let's instead stir
our marriage with teaspoons.

The *Times'* headlines juice our mornings.
If your teacup slips into argument,
if tea spills through cracks in the cup

and overflows the Limoges, remember
every broken cup is a treasure.
Let's repair bone china in the evening.

The Red Dress

She wore a red dress the last time we met,
linen, I think.

With my eyes I lifted the hem of the fabric
so my gaze looked on her white limbs.

The cut was ordinary, on her hips
flax swam like a dolphin, leaping high

into the air, splashing curves
wherever she walked.

We didn't think our luck
would ever run out

until my wife discovered her
stuck to a photograph of mine.

I will never see her red dress unzip
and fall to the floor again.

Last Dragon in Chinatown

Fall flames rust red as an aging dragon exits,
an ice blue mouse breathes cool air in the attic.
At home I refuse to change the light bulbs

in the ceiling, afraid I'll fall
from the ladder and land in a bowl of soup.
I can swim, but can't untangle the noodles.

How do I light up my life in December?
By finding a young lover who needs experience?
Or an older companion who wants assurance?

Both are sweet bon-bons for a rheumatic
dragon who rummages in cedar closets
and finds plastic snakes and two dollar umbrellas.

I stop breathing fire and sigh fidelity again.
My eardrums are inflamed with worldly gossip
exchanged with fish and fruit store salesman.

This time I should look for happy wives.
At Columbus Park chattering women leave
mah-jong tables, go home to cook dinner.

Under the shade of a gingko tree,
I find an empty bench. Like a squirrel,
I tear open a package of treats.

A stranger joins me and smiles.
A pair of red wings unfold over my head. The hairy
legs of a giant butterfly carry me to Cathay.

In That Dank Womb of Happiness

We swim like blind fish, antennae probing
ceilings for escape hatches. I scratch
in search of blue skies above the cavern.

Lost after fifty years, I wonder was I right
to probe and feel for answers, to say,
tell me the truth, are we fit for one another?

There is no answer. I sleep in the bed
we make, the reply comes quietly as we
snore, and I curve into her hip.

ACKNOWLEDGMENTS

Atlanta Review, "Tea with Milosz"

Inkwell, "Dirty Pictures"

Margie, "Self Portrait of an Aging Artist" and "Stalin's Mustache"

Mudfish Review, "Fish Ball Soup and Flowers"

North American Review, "On the Jersey Turnpike I Stopped to Pee at the Walk Whitman Service Center"

Tikkun, "East Side Dyubbuk"

"The Red Dress" was winner of *Mississippi Review*'s 2011 Poetry Prize.

www.ingramcontent.com/pod-product-compliance
Lightning Source LLC
Chambersburg PA
CBHW031150090426
42738CB00008B/1285